beadalicious

beadalicious

25 Fresh, Unforgettable Jewelry Projects for Beads Old and New

SONYA NIMRI

Photographs by Carrie Grim
Illustrations by Dany Paragouteva

WATSON-GUPTILL PUBLICATIONS, NEW YORK

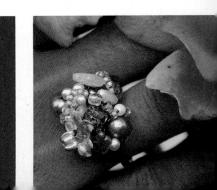

SENIOR ACQUISITIONS EDITOR: Julie Mazur
EDITOR: Amy Vinchesi
DESIGNER: L49 Design
PRODUCTION MANAGER: Alyn Evans

Text copyright © 2008 by Sonya Nimri
Illustrations copyright © 2008 by Dany Paragouteva
Photographs copyright © 2008 by Carrie Grim

First published in 2008 by Watson-Guptill Publications,
Nielsen Business Media, a division of The Nielsen
Company, 770 Broadway, New York, NY 10003
www.watsonguptill.com

Library of Congress Cataloging-in-Publication Data
Nimri, Sonya.
  Beadalicious : 25 fresh, unforgettable jewelry projects
for beads old and new / Sonya Nimri ; photography by
Carrie Grim ; illustrations by Dany Paragouteva.
    p. cm.
  Includes index.
  ISBN-13: 978-0-8230-9996-2 (pbk. : alk. paper)
  ISBN-10: 0-8230-9996-2 (pbk. : alk. paper)
  1. Beadwork. 2. Jewelry making. I. Title.
  TT860.N550 2008
  745.58'2--dc22

                    2007036414

Printed in Singapore

First printing, 2008

1 2 3 4 5 6 7 8 9 / 15 14 13 12 11 10 09 08 07

This book is dedicated to mon Chank,
who be killin', and to Olaf, who resembles a
conglomerate of gray pearls himself.

contents

INTRODUCTION 8

THE UNBEADABLE BASICS 10

the ingredients 12
the techniques 26

introduction

BEADALICIOUS is different from any other beading book out there—it is an explosion of eye-catching, fresh, totally unique jewelry pieces put together with beads old and new.

The origins of this book lie in two passions of mine. First and foremost, I am a lover of style. I like fashion that makes a statement while still being timeless and wearable. Trends come and go, but I find that certain designs are eternally pleasing to the eye. This is just as true for jewelry as it is for clothes, and the projects here reflect my love of novel, lively, playful style.

Another big passion is giving old and existing materials an updated life. In my first book, Just for the Frill of It, the victims were old, dated clothes, which I transformed into treats full of texture and fun. In Beadalicious, that same energy comes to jewelry. I love to recycle beads and reuse materials like wire, glass, clay, wood, and shells. For me, it's the challenge of reusing everyday objects that makes jewelry-making the most rewarding. To see the old and dilapidated in an updated setting is to stretch the mind and give way to creativity.

Beads come in colors and textures as lush and varied as ripe fruit. And while this book *is* a technical guide, it should be used above all as a source of inspiration. If you can't find the same charms I used for the Long John Silver necklace, use whichever ones catch your fancy. If your craft store doesn't carry the same shaped punches used in the Goodnight Moon necklace, use different ones and make yours unique. The Cat Lady necklace can be made with any filigreed cameo out there. You can buy new beads that closely match the ones I used or replace them with whatever you have.

Beads are endlessly expressive, and the choices you make in combining them lead to infinite possibilities. Mix a luminous apricot seed bead with milky-white glass chunks and glistening dark brown leather for a fantastically rich combination. Combine a gold filigree bead with a brown wooden bead to say "antique rustic," or put the same gold bead with a hot-pink stone for something lively and trendy. As countless as there are tastes in the world, there are beading combinations that will make mouths water and heads turn.

The skills needed to make the projects in this book are very basic. **If you can hold a pair of pliers and count to fifty, you can master any technique in this book.** The wire-wrapping projects, like the Queen of Hearts necklace on page 78, take a bit more patience but in the end are beautiful and timeless works of art.

Don't be scared to explore and try your own version of anything in this book. There are no rules when it comes to creativity.

HOW HARD IS IT?

Each project in this book has been given a difficulty rating, so you can see in advance what to expect. Here's what the ratings mean:

mild

Like squeezing an orange—with a little effort, anyone can do it. These projects require opening and closing jump rings and making simple loops with wire.

medium

Easy enough if you measure carefully, like baking an instant cake. These will involve slightly more difficult wire techniques, such as wrapping and "pigtailing."

cajun

Mamacita! These projects are a bit more involved. Follow the directions closely and set aside enough time so you don't feel rushed.

Note: Beads are like little mouth-watering treats for the eye. In the spirit of celebrating their deliciousness, I also paired each project with a recipe it seemed to inspire. Some are to eat or drink, others to pour into your bath or scent your lingerie drawer—but all will inspire your senses. Gathered from friends, family, and my own experimentation, I recommend them all!

the unBEADable

basics

the ingredients

Stocking your craft area is like stocking a kitchen—it's a major hassle if, in the middle of preparing a big recipe, you have to run to the store in your pajamas to get a missing ingredient.

Whatever your shopping style—whether you're a "minimalist" who only gets what you need for a specific project, a "well stocked" crafter who buys things here and there when the mood strikes, or someone who, like me, is constantly prepping for the Babette's Feast of jewelry-making, with an overflowing stockpile of beads and trinkets—you'll want to make sure you have at least the basics on hand before diving into the projects. Here's a rundown of what you'll need.

As I mentioned in the introduction, I'm a big fan of reusing old beads and giving them new life. See my ode to vintage materials on page 22. Otherwise, if you want to supplement your old stuff with new beads and findings, your local crafts store should have everything you need. I've also listed a number of resources at the back of the book, starting on page 124.

Vintage beads, like these amber beads from a 1970s neck-lace, become the focal points of a fresh, unique pair of earrings (see Amber Drops, page 40).

BEADS, BEADS, BEADS

Beads come in a gazillion different varieties and shapes. It can be a bit confusing, so here's a rundown of the major categories we will be using in this book.

Seed beads

"Seed bead" is a generic term for any small bead. Usually round and made of plastic or glass, they range in size from less than 1 mm to several millimeters in diameter and come in every color you can imagine. They are sold in every craft store, usually by the hank (strung in lengths) or in little packets. Most high-quality glass seed beads are made in either the Czech Republic or Japan. Here are some of the most common types.

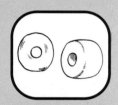
seed beads

rocaille beads

japanese seed beads

japanese cube beads

Rocaille beads. The term rocaille originally referred to round, silver-lined seed beads with a square hole, but today it covers all round seed beads with either a round or a square hole. Frequently, rocaille seed beads are not perfectly uniform, which adds to their appeal.

Some craft stores have tubs of mixed glass beads from which you can just scoop out an assortment and then pay by weight. Many of the beads on the Festival of Lanterns Bracelet (page 92) are from tubs like that.

Japanese seed beads are glass seed beads that are precisely uniform, with larger holes. They are also a bit more expensive. I prefer the irregular, cheaper rocaille beads because I like the lack of uniformity of the shapes.

Japanese cube beads are precision-made, perfectly cylindrical glass seed beads that look like tiny square tiles when woven in a pattern. They have a relatively large hole for their size, which makes them light, so you get more beads per gram. These features make them ideal for weaving projects, which I don't have the patience to do but like a whole lot.

charlotte cut beads

bugle beads

clay seed beads

cane beads

pressed beads

Charlotte cut beads are glass beads that have a cut down one side to make them appear faceted and to add sparkle.

Bugle beads are tube-shaped glass beads that come in different lengths, with holes the same size as seed beads. These beads are beautiful and work especially well for wire-wrapping projects (see the Queen of Hearts Necklace, Bohemian Wrapsody Ring, and Lucky Clover Hair Comb).

Clay seed beads are the cheapest beads in the world. They come in a range of sizes, from tiny 2-mm beads that need a delicate needle to thread them to giant ones you could run a rope through.

Glass Beads

Furnace glass beads (a.k.a. **cane beads**) are made using Italian glass-making techniques. They get their name from the fact that they require a large glass furnace and an annealing kiln to create.

They are also called "cane" beads because they are made by fusing together several colored canes of glass, which are then cut across into various shapes and sizes. The resulting beads have what look like vertical stripes because of the different-colored canes fused together. The beads can be cylindrical, square, rectangular, and triangular in shape.

Pressed beads are glass beads that have been stamped into shapes, usually leaves, flowers, or stars.

spacer beads

filigree beads

plated beads

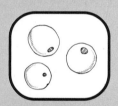

pearls

bicone swarovski crystals

Metal Beads

Spacer beads come in a variety of metallic colors (brass, copper, blackened silver, silver, and gold) and shapes and are great for balancing out rich color palettes and adding textural variety. I usually acquire these when I'm taking apart old jewelry.

Filigree beads are perfect if you want to add a luxurious, medieval feel to a piece. These patterned, hollow metal beads come in gold and silver and range from tiny, peppercorn size to those the size of large jawbreakers.

Plated beads are often gold- or silver-plated decorative beads. The more expensive, higher karat gold-plated ones look stunning when placed between colorful beads.

Other Types of Beads

Pearls, both real and fake, are my favorite beads to work with. The big ones remind me of Barbara Bush, and the little ones are so precious and delicate that I just love incorporating them in everything I can. Pearls run the gamut in cost, depending on if they are real (hundreds of dollars apiece) or plastic (a few dollars for a strand). The way to tell the difference is by rubbing one on your front tooth. If it feels smooth, it's fake; if there is a grating, sandy feel, it's real. Real pearls tend to have tiny holes that are hard to fit onto some wires and strings. There is a tool that expands the holes called a bead reamer, available at most craft stores.

Bicone Swarovski crystals, shiny, bright, glistening crystal beads from Austria, add sparkle to any project. When I find these strung on thrift-store necklaces or bracelets with other beads, I know I've totally scored. They come in a variety of shapes and sizes, and while they'll run you a bit more than glass beads, I find that a little goes a long way.

semiprecious stone chips

cloisonné beads

faceted beads

teardrop-shaped beads

briolette beads

Semiprecious stone chips are made from chips of semiprecious stones, and they are available in a range of shapes and sizes. I like using these in the wire-wrapping projects because they are still beautiful stones but less expensive than the refined or polished varieties.

Cloisonné beads are named for the ancient Chinese wiring and enameling process used to make these beautiful, delicate enamel beads. I used cloisonné beads in the Festival of Lanterns Bracelet, the Bright Pretty Things Lariat, and the Pearl Duster Earrings.

Faceted beads are any beads that have been cut multiple times in different directions for maximum sparkle. They have a symmetrical look, and jewelry made with them tends to look classy and *très cher*. Two-cut beads are cut, or faceted, in two places; three-cut beads in three places. Triangle-cut beads are three sided. Hexagonal are six-sided seed beads that look faceted. Faceted beads come in anything from plastic to crystal—it's the cut that defines them.

Teardrop-shaped beads are perfectly rounded drop beads that have a horizontal hole going through the top of the bead. **Briolette beads** are shaped like flattened teardrops, with a blunt bottom. They are often used to dangle loosely off the bottom of pieces. These come in a variety of materials, from precious stones to plastic.

Sometimes you may think you have a great idea for combining bead colors and textures, but the final result ends up looking . . . off. Why put all the work into something you'll never wear? Always test your choices before stringing them. The easiest way to do this is to take a small, shallow, neutral-colored dish—like the larger half of a mint tin—and put a small sampling of the beads in it. Swirl them around for an even distribution. You will see right away which beads stand out. Swap those with others you think might work better as complements. Do this until you see balance and harmony in your tin.

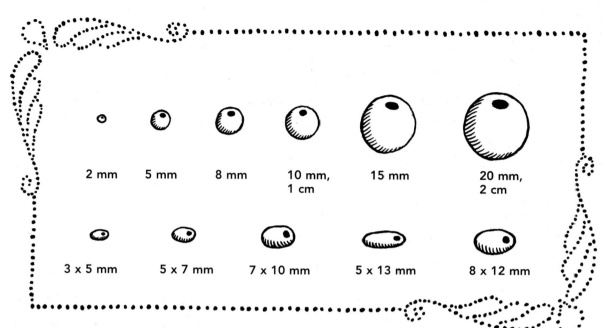

2 mm   5 mm   8 mm   10 mm, 1 cm   15 mm   20 mm, 2 cm

3 x 5 mm   5 x 7 mm   7 x 10 mm   5 x 13 mm   8 x 12 mm

Beads range in size from nearly microscopic to very large.
This chart will give you a feel for the sizes used in this book.

rhinestone beads

wooden beads

plastic beads

Rhinestone beads are made of (what else!) rhinestones set in metal discs and are perfect for adding a touch of bling.

Wooden beads are made from any type of wood and are available in a range of colors, from natural to stained bright hues. They're often sold individually. My favorite wooden beads, and a common type, are cedar beads. They smell great for a long time (as long as you don't go into a Jacuzzi with them on).

Plastic beads are cheap fun. They're a great find in the vintage section of a shop or in a big value-pack, one-pound bag. I like to combine them with glass and pearls for the juxtaposition of textures.

polymer clay beads

bone and horn beads

buttons

shells

seeds

Polymer clay beads can be made to mimic the look of any other material, from metal to porcelain to glass. Check out a book on making polymer clay beads and create your own unique colors and textures.

Bone and horn beads are carved out of actual animal bones and have a great rustic, natural look. There are also plastic versions that closely resemble the real thing.

Unconventional Beads

You might be surprised at what can be used as a bead. Pretty much anything with a hole in it will work!

Buttons can be a perfect stand-in for beads. I have a large jar of vintage buttons from Mrs. Copeland, a gentle lady who passed away a while ago. Some of them are real ivory, which is rare and illegal now (for good reason). I used some of them in the Old-Time Button Headband and Long John Silver Necklace.

Shells from souvenir necklaces, thrift stores, hanging plant holders, and owl wall hangings are another good addition. Even Karl Lagerfeld used shells in a recent Chanel Couture collection. One thing to remember is that they do tend to be more appropriate for spring and summer jewelry, what with their associations with hot Jamaican nights and learning to surf on Waikiki Beach.

Seeds can be another good addition to your bead bin. It is so easy to make beads out of lemon seeds—just stick a large needle through the seed and let it dry for a few days. Seeds are not your everyday material, but their unusual texture can add interest to a piece, and they're surprisingly durable. I used seeds in the Queen of Hearts and Long John Silver necklaces.

Beachcombers can turn a seashell of any size or shape into a one-of-a-kind showpiece, like this Sparkles on a Half Shell necklace (see page 88).

fabric cutouts

Fabric cutouts, such as those made of felt, are colorful, soft, and can add an inexpensive but dramatic note of color and texture. I bought scrapbooking punches and punched shapes out of felt for the beads in my Goodnight Moon Necklace.

CHAINS

Chains aren't only for bracelets and necklaces—they're also a fun way to add texture to any beading project. I love using them as tassels or layering them in sheets for a stand-alone project. Chain types are as varied as beads. They come in a range of colors, link styles, and widths. I've listed a few of the major types.

dapper bar chain

Dapper bar chains have flattened bars with holes at each end connected by oblong jump rings. I use this type of chain the most in my projects because of its uniqueness and elegance.

Cable chains have regular links that are all exactly the same size and oval shape. These are simple, timeless chains that work for many projects.

cable chain

Elongated cable chains have longer, oblong links. These are another attractive type of chain, but they're not great for adding charms to as the links turn vertical with the weight of anything hanging from them.

Curb chains have links that are all tweaked to one side, in the same direction. Curb chains can range in thickness, from delicate and feathery to heavy-duty, lock-up-your-bicycle. The links also come in different lengths, from small and round to elongated. I find this style a bit more punk rock industrial.

elongated cable chain

Figaro chains (as in *The Marriage of . . .*) have a repeating pattern of three same-size tweaked links followed by a fourth, elongated tweaked link. I'm not sure why they are called Figaro chains; apparently the design was invented in Italy, but I pretty much only see them in the States. I'm not crazy about the Figaro as a straight chain, but I quite like it in the Long John Silver Necklace.

curb chain

figaro chain

box chain

jump rings

head pins

eye pins

crimp beads

bead caps

Box chains have links shaped like boxes that hook together, giving them a serpentine look. Box chains were popular for jewelry made in the '80s and were perfect for my Mystery Owl Bookmark project.

JEWELRY FINDINGS

Jewelry findings are the hardware that hold your pieces together. Like the yeast that makes home-baked bread rise, they are essential to a successful outcome.

Jump rings are the best way to connect jewelry and can be picked up at any crafts or beading store for just a few dollars per bunch. They range from 2 to 6 mm in inner diameter; it's a good idea to have a few sizes on hand. The projects in this book use 4-mm rings, except where noted otherwise.

Head pins are pieces of wire with a flat, round head at one end. They are usually sold in either 20 or 22 gauge and in lengths ranging from 1 to 3 inches. The projects in this book all use 2-inch, 20-gauge head pins.

Eye pins are just like head pins but with a round loop at one end instead of the flat head. They're perfect for projects with tassels, like the Black & White Balls Earrings, Festival of Lanterns Bracelet, and Bright, Pretty Things Lariat. They are sold in either 20 or 22 gauge and lengths ranging from 1 to 3 inches. I used the 2-inch, 22-gauge size throughout.

Crimp beads are strung onto the end of a line of beads and then flattened to grip the wire and hold the beads in place. They come in four sizes, ranging from .25 mm to .91 mm.

Bead caps are supposed to be used as ornamental caps on beads, to embellish a plain bead of the same size. But they're so pretty that I use them on their own, too, sometimes dropping them wrong-side down, like a blooming flower.

mining the old stuff:
GOING VINTAGE

The materials you need to make the projects in this book—or any jewelry, really—can certainly be bought new. But if you're like me, you'll get even more pleasure out of reusing, rediscovering, and revamping old jewelry. This is the stuff forgotten in attics and changing hands in thrift stores everywhere. You may not find the exact same bead or material used in each project, but that just means yours will be that much more unique!

Recently, a pile of my Grandma Bobby's old jewelry landed in my lap. Pearls, clunky wooden beads, "golver" (not gold . . . but not quite silver, either) pins and chokers—it all looked sort of lonely and dated but was soaked with memories of a beautiful woman who led a happy life. When I held her necklace of gigantic amber beads and blue-stained wooden discs (a combination that definitely needed breaking up), I thought, "She must have been a free spirit to wear this concoction, because I couldn't even rock this one to the car wash." I ended up recombining the beads in my own style, but her fun, lively energy will survive because they will be worn with thoughts of her. This is the beauty and versatility of vintage jewelry: it holds memories while serving as an empty palate, ready to start a new life.

The key to culling vintage jewelry is learning to look beyond the jewelry's present, dated composition to see its unique, independent elements. So what if a necklace was styled to wow the 1975 potluck crowd? It may be made of materials with unusual colors and rare designs quite unlike the mass-produced jewelry you see in stores today. Multiple strands of pearls, clunky plastic bead necklaces, heavy "golver" chains and brooches, tons of rhinestones—they may look pretty silly in their present state, but learn to peer deeper into the DNA of a piece. Each bead, clasp, and pendant has a personality independent from how it has been presented. Could the strands of cheap plastic beads combine with semiprecious stones, glass beads, and sequins for a new look? Is the chain reusable? If the chain has a weird kink in it, could you just cut out the problem area and use it for something smaller, like a bunch of bracelets, earrings, or even a purse handle? And don't forget to look at findings, like the clasp: Is it a well-made vintage lock-and-key toggle clasp that could be reused? If there is one thing that should be collected from old jewelry, it is findings—they are the staples that can be used over and over in many projects.

Once you get the hang of dissecting, evaluating, and reformulating jewelry into something new, the possibilities become endless. And best of all, it's outrageously fun. It's like being a visual chemist, magician, or sorceress—a wiggle of the nose and it all comes together. Don't worry about messing up, either. You can always form another all-star cast with a snap of your fingers. The creations you compose are an affirmation of your creativity, cleverness, and independence. The key is to approach each vintage piece with a fresh eye and to look at all the possibilities, even those that seem silly and frivolous at first. With a little imagination, that which is unsightly and laughable can become fresh and hip.

WHERE TO HUNT FOR VINTAGE JEWELRY

THRIFT STORES AND GARAGE SALES

I'm always up for a bargain, and there is no better place to get one than a garage sale or thrift store. I once purchased a huge bag of junk jewelry for a dollar. At Goodwill, I found a faded tank-top with chains draped across the front; I used the chains for the Chain Reaction Earrings on page 50. Broken necklaces are great for their findings (clasps) and chains, and old pins for the pin backings and miscellaneous jewels. Beaded bracelets are great to take apart, too.

FRIENDS AND THEIR GRANDMOTHERS

You wouldn't believe the amount of jewelry that will start coming your way when you tell people you'll take their old stuff. Even the worst, oxidized, chipped plastic pearls can look *très chic* when partnered with the right things (check out the Cat Lady necklace on page 82). When people give you their precious leftovers, don't pick through them in front of them and leave what you don't want. Take it all and graciously thank them. When you get home you can gag, laugh, and throw out or give away the ridiculous, but do so at your peril! Sometimes things you think are terrible end up being exactly the right thing to complete a piece. I'm just saying. This is why I save everything.

RETIRED SCHOOL TEACHERS

Every teacher I know has an unusually large collection of costume jewelry. Do students bring them jewelry as presents? Or is it just a teacher thing? I have no idea, but it's a real trend. Trust me.

YOUR CHILDHOOD STASH

I still use beads I collected when I was little. Costume jewelry, plastic beads, souvenir anklets, turquoise chips—I use all of it now.

pin back

earwires

lobster clasp

toggle clasp

wire

plastic-coated wire

Pin backs turn a beaded object into a pin. Sometimes they have sticky tape on the back to adhere to a flat surface, but I prefer the ones without tape since I often adhere them to non-flat surfaces.

Earwires are used to create dangling earrings. They range in style from elegant, simple hooks to sturdy lever clasps; the most common is shaped like a fishing hook.

Clasps are used to close a necklace or bracelet. There are many types: my favorites are the **lobster clasp** and **toggle clasp**. Lobster clasps come in various sizes, from tiny 8 mm to a giant 16-mm claw you could serve with butter and lemon! Toggle clasps come in large sizes only, so they are best for meaty, heavier pieces. A third type is the hook-and-eye clasp, which comes in some fun patterns.

OTHER MATERIALS

Wire comes in different gauges; ironically, the higher the number the thinner the wire. I use only three gauges of wire in this book: 18-gauge for the sturdy armature of the wire-wrapped projects, 24-gauge for wrapping and the more heavily beaded projects, and the lighter 32-gauge in the Pearl Duster Earrings.

Plastic-coated wire is a tough, pliable, plastic-coated spiral wire and is available in various brands and sizes.

leather cord

round-nose pliers

flat-nose pliers

wire cutters

Leather cord can be another great material. I have a spool of natural-colored, 1.5-mm leather cord that came in handy for the Queen of Hearts Necklace. It feels comfortable, and the natural color goes with anything.

TOOLS

Happily, there aren't many tools you need to become a world-class jewelry master, and the ones you do need aren't expensive. There are three tools you cannot live without and a few more that will certainly make your life easier if you have them on hand.

The Trifecta of Must-Haves

Round-nose pliers are *muy importante* and just what they sound like—pliers whose tips are rounded. Good round-nose pliers are essential to making a perfectly round wire loop.

Flat-nose pliers (also called needle-nose or chain-nose pliers) are like little jaws for grabbing wire and jump rings. They are great for getting a firm grip on wire and for closing loop ends. They are also indispensable for bending wire and holding it steady while wrapping with another tool.

Wire cutters come in two types: Jeweler's wire cutters have pointed ends for getting into tight spots, and fine, sharp blades for cutting delicate wire. These are essential for finishing your loops and trimming excess wire or chain ends. Heavy-duty cutters are only needed for cutting very thick wire—18-gauge and below. The only projects in this book that require a heavy-duty cutter are the Reigning Precious Tiara, Bohemian Wrapsody Ring, and Lucky Clover Hair Comb.

crimping pliers

beading awl

bent-nose pliers

Can-Live-Withouts

Crimping pliers are used to curl and then flatten crimp beads. These aren't critical—sometimes I use flat-nose pliers instead—but crimping pliers will make the curving much smoother, your work will look more professional, and there won't be any sharp edges for the person wearing the jewelry.

A beading awl is a tool with a long shaft that tapers into a point, sort of like an ice pick. It is used to guide the hole of a knot toward the bead. You could use a toothpick for this as well.

Bent-nose pliers are bent at the end for getting in really close to the wire when beads or a loop are in the way. They're useful but not critical.

the techniques

There are only a few techniques you need to learn to make the projects in this book, but it's worthwhile getting them down so you can do them smoothly and quickly while working on a project. Here's a crash course.

OPENING AND CLOSING JUMP RINGS

Jump rings are ubiquitous in beading, and it's important to know how to open and close them without mangling their circular shape.

1. In one hand, use a pair of flat-nose pliers to firmly hold the jump ring at one side of the split opening.

2. In the other hand, use another pair of

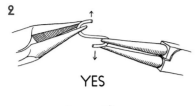

pliers (round-nose pliers are fine) to bend the other side of the ring away from you. Never open the sides wide from left to right, like a mouth, or you will deform the circular shape.

3. To close a jump ring, do the same and bend the ring back in toward you until the sides meet again.

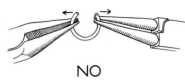

NO

WORKING WITH HEAD PINS AND EYE PINS

Making a Simple Loop

Every time you want to attach a head or eye pin to something else, you'll need to roll the thin end of the pin into a little loop. It takes a bit of practice to get a perfect loop, but after you've got it it's like riding a bicycle: you'll never forget.

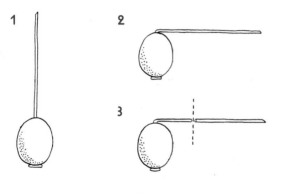

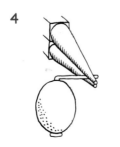

1. Stack your bead(s) on the pin against the flat end. Leave at least half an inch of the pin sticking out at the top; beads should not be stacked to the top of the pin.

2. Use your fingers to bend the exposed pin against the bead at a right angle.

3. Use wire cutters to snip the excess pin, leaving ¼ to ½ inch, depending on how large you want your loop. (Save the extra piece and use it to measure how much to cut off your next pin, so both are the same.)

4. Grasp the exposed tip with your round-nose pliers.

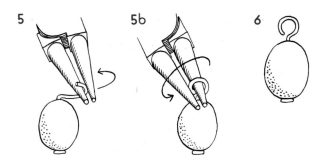

5. Roll the tip into a circle by rotating your wrist. To complete the rotation, release the wire and readjust your grip. Make sure to place your pliers back on the pin at the same spot. Continue to roll the pin until it is a complete loop.

6. Use wire cutters to trim any excess pin.

Making a Loop with a Triple Wrap, a.k.a. "Pigtailing"

This is a sturdier loop that will ensure beads on the pin will not slip off. It's also quite decorative; the triple wrap makes the loop look finished and professional. I call this technique "pigtailing" because the wire wrapped around the stem looks like a little piggy's curled tail.

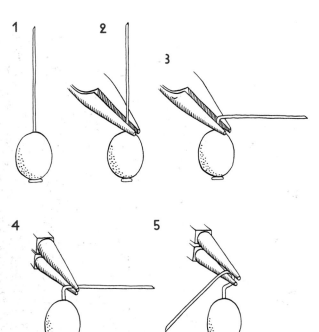

1. Stack your bead(s) onto a head pin against the flat end. The other end of the pin should be sticking out the top by about half an inch.

2. Use flat-nosed pliers to grasp the exposed pin just above the beads.

3. With your fingers, bend the wire at a right angle over the pliers.

4. Use a pair of round-nose pliers to grasp the wire above the bend. Use your fingers to bend the wire up and over the top jaw, about 180 degrees.

5. The top jaw of the round-nose pliers is now inside the loop. Release the wire and

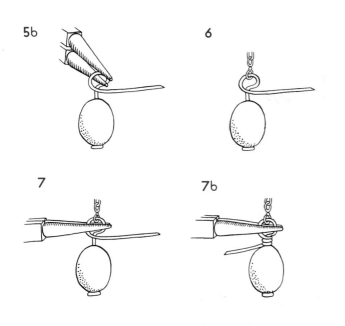

5b

6

7

7b

adjust the pliers so the bottom jaw is inside the loop. Then use your fingers to bend the wire under and around the bottom jaw, about 180 degrees.

6. Let go of the loop. If you are attaching a chain or another loop, slip it on now.

7. Grasp the loop from the side with needle-nose pliers. Bend wire to a 90-degree angle, then use your fingers to wrap the tail tightly around the stem three times.

8. Use wire cutters to clip off any excess wire.

8

"Pigtailing" is a technique used throughout the book to elegant effect, such as in this Bright Pretty Things Lariat (on page 68).

Adding a knot between each bead keeps them in place and regularly spaced (see Tree of Life necklace on page 70).

The Briolette Wrap

This is a technique for wrapping a briolette or pear-shaped bead, though it can be used on any bead that needs to be dropped as a pendant.

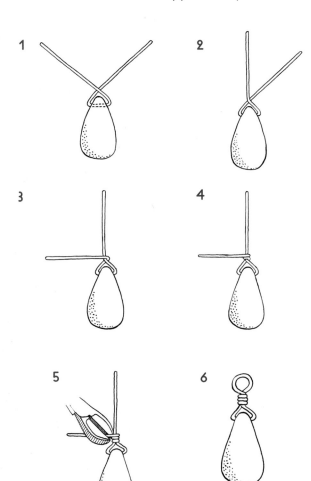

1. Put a 6-inch piece of 24-gauge wire through the hole in a briolette bead. Cross one side over the other.

2. Use flat-nose pliers to bend one wire so that it points straight up from the tip of the briolette.

3. Begin to wrap the other wire by crossing it over the straight one. Wrap the wire around one full rotation.

4. Wrap the wire another three times around the straight wire.

5. Use wire cutters to clip off any excess from the wrapped wire.

6. Using your round-nose pliers, wrap the remaining wire into a loop.

DECORATIVE TECHNIQUES

Knotting between Beads

If you are stringing beads onto a leather, silk, or nylon cord, you may wish to add a knot between each bead. This adds a nice decorative touch and keeps the bead securely in place.

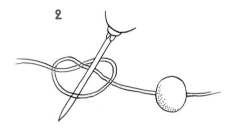

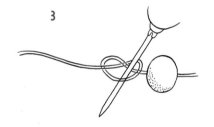

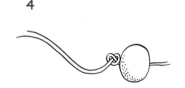

1. String a bead onto your cord.

2. Tie a loose overhand knot. Insert an awl or toothpick into the loop.

3. Use the awl to pull the knot as close to the bead as possible.

4. Remove the awl or toothpick from the knot and tighten.

5. Repeat steps 1–4 between each bead.

Adding Chain Tassels

Tassels make everything more interesting. They add movement and texture to what might otherwise be too many curves of bulbous parts. Plus, they give you something to swing around!

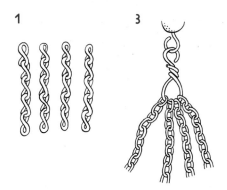

1. Cut a chain into several equal pieces of whatever length you want your tassel to be.

2. Make a U with some wire and place 4 or 5 chain pieces on it.

3. Wire-wrap the loop according to the pigtailing directions on page 28 and attach to your earring wire.

CLOSING A NECKLACE OR BRACELET

Finishing the Ends of a Cord with a Loop

Before stringing up a leather necklace, make a loop at one end for a clasp to hook onto for the closure. This is more attractive than adding a jump hoop.

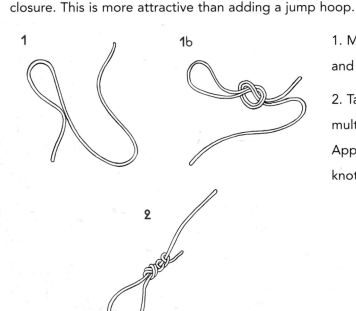

1. Make a loop at one end of your cord and knot it.

2. Take the loose end of the cord and tie it multiple times around the rest of the cord. Apply a generous amount of glue to the knot to secure.

Making Your Own Toggle Clasp

Here's how to make your own toggle clasp on a two-strand cord.

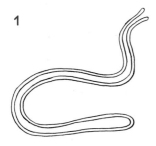

1

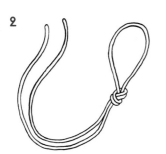

2

1. Take your length of cord and double it.

2. Tie the folded end into a knot, making a loop about ½ inch long.

3. Choose a bead that fits through the loop somewhat snugly. String both loose ends of the cord through the bead and secure the bead between two knots so it won't slip around.

4. To fasten, pull the bead through the loop. When you wear the piece, the tension will hold the clasp in place.

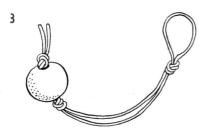

3

4

Looping the ends of leather cord in this Old-Time Button Headband is an important step in securing the elastic (see page 112).

earrings

fresh cherry drops

Every year I look forward to cherry season, usually mid-May through mid-June. I always try to do a fresh cherry and strawberry taste test, to decide which crop turned out better that year. Lately, the cherries have been winning. The best are the California Bings when they're fresh from the farm. There are even farms where you can go play farm girl for the day and pick your own. Note to self: Wear these earrings for that excursion.

RECYCLED ELEMENT: Ribbon from a gift

1 AND 2

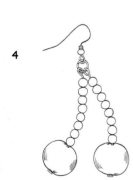

4

1. Take a head pin and slide on a red bead, then 8 jade beads. Gently bend the pin slightly so it looks like a curved stem.

2. Using the round-nose pliers, make a loop at the top of the stem.

3. Repeat steps 1 and 2 for the second stem.

4. Attach both stems to a jump ring. Connect the jump ring to the earwire.

5. Cut a 6-inch length of ribbon and make a bow around the front of the earwire.

6. Add a dab of glue to the back of the bow in a few spots so it doesn't come undone.

7. Repeat steps 1–6 for the second earring.

INGREDIENTS

 4 round, red 2-cm beads
32 round, dark green jade 5-mm beads
Thin ivory satin ribbon, 12 inches long
 4 gold head pins
 2 gold jump rings
 2 gold earwires
G-S Hypo Cement or Super Glue

TOOLS

Flat-nose pliers
Round-nose pliers
Wire cutters

CHERRY LIP JELLY

Here is a quick recipe for a sweet-tasting lip balm to give out as a gift or to use yourself. Pucker up!

2½ teaspoons beeswax
 7 teaspoons sweet almond oil
 1 teaspoon honey
 1 capsule vitamin E
 5 drops cherry essential oil
 Small, clean container with lid

Heat the oil and beeswax in a little saucepan over low heat until the beeswax is completely melted. Remove from heat. Add the honey and whisk it all together. When the mixture is nearly cool, add the cherry essential oil. Mix again and then pour into your lip balm container. Leave at room temperature to cool completely.

pearl dusters

I love these earrings because they so delicately brush upon the shoulders, like wisps of feathery lightness. They remind me of tassels that hang from the bottom of a fan or a Chinese lantern, and they will add a feminine elegance to anything you wear.

RECYCLED ELEMENT: Chain from a broken necklace

INGREDIENTS

2   Chinese doughnut cloisonné beads
2   2-mm pearl beads
2   4-mm jade beads
6   4-mm pink freshwater pearls
Delicate gold chain, 12 inches long (I used a cable chain)
2   gold eye pins
2   gold earwires
32-gauge wire, 12 inches long

TOOLS

Flat-nose pliers
Round-nose pliers
Wire cutters

3

1. Take your chain and cut it into 6 equal pieces, each 2 inches long.

2. Do the same with the wire, cutting it into six 2-inch pieces.

3. Using the 2-inch pieces of wire, attach a freshwater pearl to the bottom of each piece of chain, using the briolette wrap technique.

4. Take an eye pin and use pliers to open the looped end. Slide 3 chain pieces onto the loop. Close the looped end.

4, 5, AND 6

5. Stack 3 beads on the eye pin in this order: jade bead, doughnut cloisonné bead, pearl bead.

6. Make a single loop at the top end of the eye pin and attach it to the base of an earwire. Trim the excess pin.

7. Repeat steps 4–6 for the second earring.

SHAVED ICE WITH TROPICAL FRUIT AND COCONUT SYRUP

This is a cool, sultry treat for a a hot summer night. Makes 4 servings.

½   cup grated or crumbled dark brown sugar
2   14-oz cans unsweetened coconut milk (do not shake)
2   ripe mangoes, cut into ¼-inch chunks
1   pound firm, ripe papaya, cut into ¼-inch chunks
½   pineapple, peeled, cored, and cut into ¼-inch chunks
Pinch of salt
2   cups shaved ice
4   sprigs fresh mint

1. Bring brown sugar, salt, and ¼ cup water to a simmer in a small saucepan, stirring until sugar is dissolved. Let simmer until slightly thickened, about 5 minutes.

2. Open the cans of coconut milk and scoop out ¾ cup of the thick cream from the tops only. Whisk the cream into the syrup until combined.

3. Chill syrup until cold, about 1 hour.

4. Spoon 3 tablespoons syrup into each of 4 glasses, then divide the fruit among them. Top with shaved ice and a sprig of mint.

amber drops

Amber is fossilized resin and is said to bring good fortune to whoever wears it. It might be a good idea to whip up a pair of these super-easy earrings the next time you need a little extra luck—say, for a dream job interview, a big date, or to hit the stage for a battle of the bands.

FOUND ELEMENT: Amber beads from a vintage 1970s necklace

1. Use wire cutters to cut the chain into 6 segments as follows: two 5-inch pieces, two 3-inch pieces, and two 2½-inch pieces.

2

2. Take a head pin and snip off the flat head. Pigtail one end to make a loop.

3

3. Get the chain segments. Slide one end of a 5-inch chain onto the body of the head pin, followed by a 3-inch chain, then a 2½-inch chain. Now slide on the amber bead. Finish by sliding on the opposite ends of the chains in reverse order: the 2½-inch chain, the 3-inch chain, the 5-inch chain.

4. Pigtail the other end of the head pin and trim any excess.

5

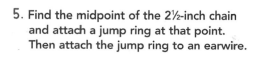

5. Find the midpoint of the 2½-inch chain and attach a jump ring at that point. Then attach the jump ring to an earwire.

6. Repeat steps 2–5 for the second earring.

INGREDIENTS

2   1¼-inch amber beads, ½ inch wide
Gold chain, 21 inches long (I used a dapper bar chain)
2   2- to 3-inch gold head pins
2   gold earwires
2   3-mm gold jump rings

TOOLS

Round-nose pliers
Flat-nose pliers
Wire cutters

RICH AMBER CARAMEL POPCORN

Caramel popcorn is an amber treat with a gooey yet gloriously crunchy texture. Eating this hands-on snack while wearing your elegant earrings will make you look like an interesting cross between a football fan and a garden tea party princess.

3   packages unbuttered microwave popcorn
2   sticks salted butter
2   cups brown sugar, firmly packed
½   cup light corn syrup
1   teaspoon baking soda
½   teaspoon cream of tartar

1. Preheat oven to 200 degrees.

2. Microwave popcorn according to directions on package. When it's done, pick out uncooked kernels. Place popcorn in a large, oven-safe bowl.

3. In a saucepan over medium heat, combine butter, brown sugar, and corn syrup and bring to a low boil for 5 minutes. Remove from heat.

4. Mix in the baking soda and cream of tartar. It will swell up momentarily and then die down again.

5. Pour the mixture over your popcorn and stir well.

6. Heat in the oven for 1 hour at 200 degrees.

purple power

Purple has been one of my favorite colors since 1984, when Prince brought the jewel tone to the height of fashion with his movie *Purple Rain*. I wasn't old enough to see the movie, but the poster had a huge influence on my fashion sense and future wardrobe. Here I've taken my version of purple raindrops and made a jewelry accessory fit for a princess.

RECYCLED ELEMENTS: Teardrop beads from a chandelier, chain from a broken necklace, gold beads from a thrift-store bracelet

INGREDIENTS

2 2.5-cm amethyst-colored teardrop beads with horizontal hole

2 amethyst-colored 5-mm seed beads

2 red heart-shaped 6-mm beads with vertical hole

2 2-cm gold connector beads (beads with loops on both sides)

Thin gold chain, 1 inch long

2 1.5-cm gold filigree bead caps

4 gold head pins

2 gold earring hoops, 1¼-inch in diameter

2 clip-on earring backs with holes in the front (I used clip-ons because these earrings are a bit heavy)

24-gauge wire, 3 inches long

TOOLS

Flat-nose pliers

Wire cutters

1

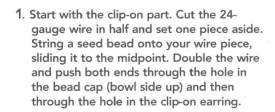

2

4, 5, AND 6

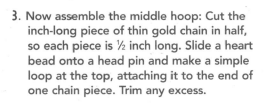

1. Start with the clip-on part. Cut the 24-gauge wire in half and set one piece aside. String a seed bead onto your wire piece, sliding it to the midpoint. Double the wire and push both ends through the hole in the bead cap (bowl side up) and then through the hole in the clip-on earring.

2. Wrap the doubled wire around the space between the bead cap and the earring back to tighten. Tuck wire ends away safely so they won't poke your earlobes.

3. Now assemble the middle hoop: Cut the inch-long piece of thin gold chain in half, so each piece is ½ inch long. Slide a heart bead onto a head pin and make a simple loop at the top, attaching it to the end of one chain piece. Trim any excess.

4. Slide your beaded chain onto one earring hoop, bringing it around to the top of the hoop and catching it in the top loop.

5. Attach the hoop to the earring clip by sliding it onto the clip elbow.

6. Open the hoop and slide a connector bead onto it. Close the hoop.

7. Attach the teardrop bead: Take a head pin and cut the flat head off. Slide it through the hole in the teardrop bead and center it. Bend both sides of the pin up, making a triangle. Make a loop with one end, looping it through the connector bead. Pigtail the other end of the pin around the stem to secure.

8. Repeat steps 1–7 for the second earring.

LAVENDER SACHET

Lavender is one of my favorite fragrances for scenting drawers and clearing my head when I have a headache. It's sort of miraculous that the little buds of lavender never dry up, but keep their oils forever. All they need is a little squeeze and the fragrance is reactivated.

½ cup lavender buds
Piece of fabric, 4 x 10 inches
Needle and thread
½-inch ribbon, 8 inches long
Pinking shears

1. Lay the fabric right-side up and fold in half lengthwise, so the "right" side is on the inside.

2. Sew two of the three open sides closed, leaving the top end open to stuff the sachet.

3. Turn the pocket right side out and fill with lavender buds.

4. Trim top edges with pinking shears and tie closed tightly with the ribbon.

black & white balls

On November 28, 1966, after the runaway success of his book *In Cold Blood*, Truman Capote hosted a legendary, star-studded party at the Plaza Hotel in New York called the Black & White Ball. Everyone was required to wear masks and dress in only black and/or white—a theme inspired by a similar ball in the 1964 movie *My Fair Lady*. Capote's guests danced the night away, drank vintage Tattinger bubbly, and munched on elegant hors d'oeuvres. Oh, how I wish I could have been there. If I had been, I would have worn a black-and-white cat mask I have from Venice, these festive, bold earrings, and an elegant black dress.

RECYCLED ELEMENTS: Giant beads from an old clunky necklace, chain from a necklace

INGREDIENTS

- 2 extra-large black round beads (I used 20-mm filigree beads)
- 4 15-mm gold filigree bead caps (for the ends of the extra-large black beads)
- 2 large black round beads (I used 15-mm beads)
- 4 5-mm black bead caps (for the ends of the large black beads)
- 2 medium-sized black round beads (I used 13-mm filigree beads)
- 2 smallish black round beads (I used 11-mm filigree beads)
- 28 flat freshwater pearls, 5-mm each
- 2 black faceted rectangular beads, 1 cm x 1.5 cm
- 14 gold eye pins
- Gold chain, 12 inches long
- 2 gold clip-on earring backs (these earrings are heavy)
- G-S Hypo Cement Glue

TOOLS

Round-nose pliers
Flat-nose pliers
Wire cutters

2

1. Take one eye pin and attach the looped end to the clip-on earring.

2. Slide the smallest black ball onto the eye pin, then make a single loop in the pin below the ball. Trim off the excess.

3

3. Get another eye pin and attach the looped end to the piece in step 2. Slide on 4 pearls and make a single loop in the pin below the pearls. Trim off the excess.

4. Do the same with a third eye pin, this time adding the medium-sized black ball, again making a single loop in the pin below the bead.

5. Repeat with a fourth eye pin strung with 4 pearls.

tip

I used large, chunky filigree beads here, but you can use ball-shaped beads of any size or color. Smaller beads will give these earrings a more elegant look, while bigger beads say fun and drama.

6. Repeat, adding the large ball with a black bead cap at each end.

7. Repeat, adding 3 pearls.

8. Repeat one last time, adding 3 pearls, the extra-large black ball with a gold bead cap at each end, then 3 more pearls.

9. Cut the gold chain into 6 pieces, each 2 inches long. These are your tassels.

10. Attach 4 tassels to the final loop and pigtail the end.

11. To finish, glue a black rectangular bead to the front of the clip-on earring.

12. Repeat steps 1–11 for the second earring.

SALT-AND-PEPPER BODY SCRUB

This grainy, all-natural scrub will leave your skin fresh and glowing for a big night at the ball.

2 tablespoons sea salt, finely ground
1 teaspoon freshly ground black pepper
2 tablespoons honey

Mix the salt and pepper in a large bowl, then stir in the honey. After you bathe, leave your skin damp and stand in the shower. Massage the mixture into your shoulders and work your way down, exfoliating your whole body. Rinse off. You should feel tingly and invigorated!

chain reaction

I often think about chain reactions in life—how chance and the choices we make lead us down a totally unique path. What if I had stayed in Paris, or studied music instead of costume design? Would my life be any different today? Thankfully, when I look at where I am now, it seems like everything happened just perfectly, and I wouldn't change it for anything. But it does make you wonder, doesn't it? This project is an ode to the chain reactions in life. May yours be full of learning and adventure!

RECYCLED ELEMENT: Chain from a thrift-store shirt

INGREDIENTS

Silver chain, 80 inches long
6 silver head pins (small enough to fit through the links of your chain)
2 silver earwires

TOOLS

Round-nose pliers
Flat-nose pliers
Wire cutters

RASPBERRY AND BANANA SHAKE

This is the ultimate shake to refresh and revive, perfect for facing any new hurdles that come up during your own chain reactions. Makes 4 servings.

1 cup raspberries
1 banana
1¼ cups plain yogurt
2–3 tablespoons honey

Add all the ingredients together in a blender and blitz until well blended.

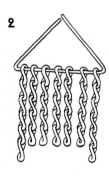

2

3

1. Start by cutting your chain into segments, as follows: 24 one-inch pieces; 4 one-inch-plus-one-link pieces; and 14 three-inch pieces. Arrange in groups according to size.

2. Take a head pin and use wire cutters to snip off the head. Slide 5 chain pieces onto the head pin in this order: 1 extra-link piece, 5 one-inch pieces, 1 extra-link piece. Center the chains on the pin. Bend the pin into a U shape, bringing both ends up in a triangle to meet in the middle.

3. Make a hanger with the points by bending one wire end straight up and making a loop at the top, attaching it to an earwire. Bend the second wire end and loop it one time around the neck of the hanger.

4

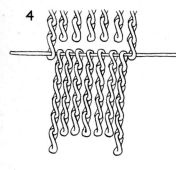

4. Now you're going to add a bar to the bottom of the chain "fringe." Pass another head pin (after snipping off the head) through the extra link on one end of the fringe. Then add 5 new chain pieces to the head pin in the same order from step 2. Finish by passing the pin through the extra-link chain at the other end.

5. Make loops at both ends of the head pin and trim the excess wire.

5

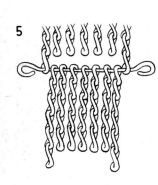

6. Add a second bar, as in step 4, this time adding 5 three-inch pieces in the middle.

7. Make loops at both ends of the head pin and trim any excess.

necklaces

goodnight moon

When I was little, my favorite bedtime book was *Goodnight Moon*. I loved looking at the moon and stars and thinking about what's in outer space. I would love to go on a tour one day, when it becomes as convenient as visiting Europe. I don't know if this will happen in my lifetime, but it sure is great to imagine. For now, I'll just dream about it while wearing this necklace.

INGREDIENTS

Packet of felt in assorted colors

Paper punches in heart, moon, and star shapes *or* precut small felt cutouts in these shapes (available at scrapbooking and/or craft stores)

Silver chain, 80 inches long

22 silver jump rings

Silver lobster clasp

White glue

TOOLS

Round-nose pliers

Flat-nose pliers

Wire cutters

RECYCLED ELEMENT: Chain from an old necklace

tip A variation on this necklace is to use charms instead of felt shapes. Just get 21 heart, moon, and star charms and add 21 more jump rings.

1

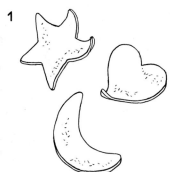

1. If you're making your own felt charms, use the shaped paper punches to punch the following shapes out of felt: 18 hearts (4 turquoise, 4 orange, 4 red, 2 white, 2 light blue, 2 pink), 6 moons (2 each in white, light blue, and mustard), and 16 stars (4 yellow, 4 purple, 4 pink, 2 orange, 2 mustard).

2. Cut off a piece of chain 14 inches long. This will be the part that goes around your neck. Attach a lobster clasp with a jump ring to one end. Attach a single jump ring to the other end.

3. Cut the rest of the chain into 21 pieces of varying lengths, following the chart below, from left to right.

CHAIN SEGMENTS IN INCHES:

1¼ 3¼ 2 3¾ 1¼ 3¾ 2¼ 4¼ 2¾ 4½ 3 5 2¾ 4½ 2¾ 4¼ 1¾ 4 1½ 3¾ 1¼

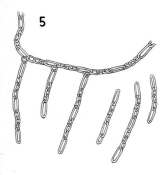

5

4. Starting 3¼ inches from one end of the 14-inch chain, attach the first piece of chain with a jump ring.

5. Move down the long chain ¼ inch and add the next piece in the chart (reading from left to right). Continue adding the pieces in order, each on a jump ring and spaced ¼ inch apart.

6. Now you're going to attach the felt shapes to the ends of the chain pieces. Take a felt shape and cover it completely with white glue. Press it to the last ¼ inch of a chain end, then back it with a second cutout in the same shape and color. You can arrange them in any order you like, or follow the order in the photo.

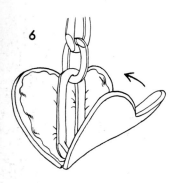

6

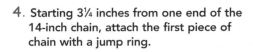

SWEET DREAMS EYE PILLOW

This soothing, aromatic eye pillow will help you drift off deliciously to sleep at night, dreaming of lavender fields.

1 clean, silky kneesock
1 cup flax seed or dry black beans
½ cup dried lavender

Fill the (hopefully clean) sock with the flax and lavender. Shake to mix and tie the end of the sock in a knot. Place on eyes at night for an enhanced dream experience.

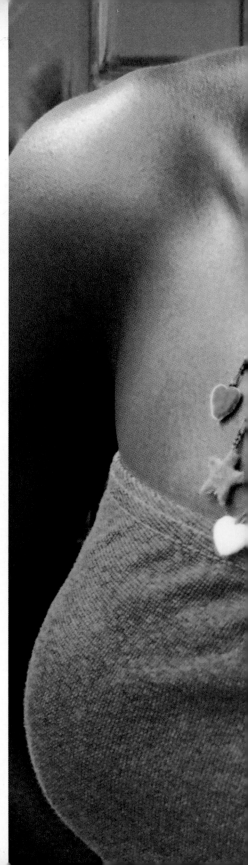

lucky charms

This is a great necklace for those who believe in the luck of talismans. I collected each of these charms from a different friend—a horseshoe, a little Scottie dog from my friend Olaf, an old scarf clip—and put them all together to make a super-lucky tiered talisman I can wear out on the town.

RECYCLED ELEMENTS: Charms, chain, and beads, all from hand-me-down jewelry

INGREDIENTS

20 green plastic beads (I used beads that range in size from .5 to 1.5 cm, but you can use beads that are all the same size if you want)

2 gold crimp beads

5–8 gold charms of varying shapes and styles (I used filigree flower bead, horseshoe charm, heart charm, branch charm, dog charm, and a filigree cameo)

Jewelry wire, 11 inches long

Medium gold chain, 12–13 inches long (I used a curb chain)

7 gold jump rings

1 small decorative toggle clasp

TOOLS

Round-nose pliers

Flat-nose pliers

Wire cutters

Crimping pliers (optional)

1. Add a crimp bead to one end of a piece of jewelry wire followed by a jump ring. Loop the wire back on itself, through the ring and back through the crimp bead. Push the crimp bead close to the end of the wire, leaving a small hoop with the jump ring. Then crimp the crimp bead just below the ring. String the 20 green beads in graduated order onto the jewelry wire. Crimp another bead with a hoop at the other end of the beaded strand.

2. Add the round half of the toggle clasp to one end with a jump ring. Attach the eye of the clasp with a jump ring to the other end.

3. Cut your chain into two pieces: one 7 inches long, the other 5 inches long. Attach the ends of both chains to the jump ring from step 2.

4. Refer to the illustration to see how the charms are linked to the necklace with jump rings.

SONYA'S LUCKY SPRING ROLLS

Trust me on this. These spring rolls are *so* tasty— and I have amazing luck after I eat them!

- 2 packets glass noodles
- 1 can garbanzo beans
- 1 cup sliced shitake mushrooms
- 1 cup diced carrots
- 1 cup diced celery
- 2 tablespoons oyster sauce

- Splash of vegetable oil
- 1 packet egg roll skins (found in the produce section of the grocery store or at Asian markets)
- 1 egg yolk, broken

1. Soak noodles in water for a few hours. Drain well.

2. Combine the veggies, oyster sauce, and noodles in a saucepan and stir-fry over medium heat until soft. Mix the noodles well until they are saturated by the sauce.

3. Add drained noodles and mix well over medium-low heat. Make sure the mixture is on the dry side and not at all saucy. Remove from heat and let cool.

4. Peel off one skin of egg roll wrapper and place on a flat surface. Add a couple of tablespoons of noodle-veggie mixture to one corner and wrap: start at the corner, then fold the sides over and roll tightly. Brush the second end with egg yolk and seal shut. Make sure the roll is nice and tight or it will fall apart in the fryer. Repeat until you've used up all the egg roll wrappers and/or veggie mixture.

5. Heat enough oil to submerge the egg rolls in a wok or large frying pan—it should be at least 3 inches deep—until bubbling hot.

6. Gently and carefully drop the egg rolls into the hot oil and fry for a few minutes, until skin is golden brown. Remove from oil using tongs, long chopsticks, or a wire wok skimmer. Place on paper towels to drain and cool before serving.

TO MAKE THE DIPPING SAUCE, whisk together the following with a fork:

- ¼ cup soy sauce
- 2 cloves garlic, crushed
- Juice of half a lemon

blossoming branch

My favorite trees are ones that produce flowers in the spring before they bear fruit. Like little heralds, they announce the new crop of fruit with their pretty, delicate presence. This necklace is an earthy rendition of a flowering branch using peachy brown tones. It looks good in so many colors—I encourage you to use your imagination!

RECYCLED ELEMENTS: Pearls, beads from an old bracelet

INGREDIENTS

5–7-mm beads (roughly 38 of them) in 4 colors (I used six 7-mm gray pearls, fifteen 5-mm taupe pearls, fifteen 5-mm plastic peach faceted beads, and five 3-mm gold beads)

24-gauge gold wire, 3 feet long

Gold lobster clasp and jump ring (to wear the branch as a choker)

Leather cord, 1½ feet long (to let the branch hang down your torso)

TOOLS

Round-nose pliers
Flat-nose pliers
Wire cutters

1

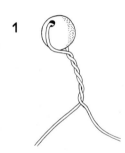

2

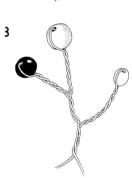

3

1. Fold the wire in half. Thread a bead onto one strand of the folded wire and slide it down to the turning point. Twist the folded wire about ½ inch below the bead, securing it in place.

2. Pull one of the wire strands out ½ inch and string on a bead in another color. Twist the wire below that bead.

3. Twist the two wires together about ¼ inch, then pull out the other wire strand and string a bead in the third color, twisting the wire below it. Twist two wires together again.

4. Add another bead 1 inch out and twist wires together until the two wires meet.

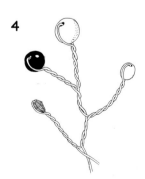

4

CHERRY BLOSSOM ICE BOWL

Ice bowls are pretty centerpieces and great for keeping their contents cool as the night wears on. Use cherry blossoms, or whatever flowers inspire you.

Fresh cherry blossoms, loose petals, and leaves
2 glass or stainless steel bowls, one slightly larger than the other

1. Fill the larger bowl about ¾ full with cold water. Add fresh blossoms, petals, and leaves.

2. Place the smaller bowl inside the large bowl, pressing down to distribute the water and flowers.

3. Weigh down the smaller bowl with some rocks or maybe a frozen burrito. You can also tape the bowls together with masking tape. Place the bowls on an even surface in the freezer and leave overnight.

3. To release the seal, run the outside of the larger bowl under lukewarm water and carefully remove the ice bowl. Keep frozen until ready to use.

7a

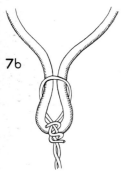

7b

5. Continue making branches with beads in alternating colors, making the length of each branch between ¼ inch and 1 inch and twisting the two wires together in between branches.

6. Continue until the beaded branch is 16 inches long.

7. Make a loop with the two wires and pigtail the ends. To wear the branch as a choker, add a lobster clasp with a jump ring; to close the lobster clasp, attach it around a larger bead at the other end. If you'd like to wear the branch hanging down your torso, as shown on page 64, run a leather cord through the loop and tie it around your neck.

bright pretty things lariat

Lariats are perhaps the easiest necklaces to make because there is no need to fasten clasps, center beads on a chain, or count links. Each end of the chain is one end of the dangling necklace, and that is all! So simple. One annoying thing about lariats is when your chain won't stay tied, so I like to use a dapper bar–style chain—it has segmented parts that catch and resist slipping.

RECYCLED ELEMENTS: Chain from a broken necklace, beads from an old bracelet

INGREDIENTS

1 20-mm faceted oval moonstone bead

1 13-mm hot-pink quartz bead

2 6-mm pink round cloisonné beads

2 9-mm gold filigree beads

2 6-mm apple-green bicone faceted crystals

Delicate gold chain (for lariat), 20–27 inches long

Gold chain (for tassels), 6 inches long

2 gold eye pins

TOOLS

Round-nose pliers

Flat-nose pliers

Wire cutters

2

3 AND **4**

1. Start by cutting the chain for your tassels into six 1-inch pieces.

2. Take an eye pin and open the looped end with your flat-nose pliers. Attach 3 chain tassels, then close the loop. Repeat with the second eye pin.

3. Take one tasseled eye pin and add beads in this order: cloisonné, moonstone, filigree, bicone crystal.

4. Make a loop at the end of the pin and attach it to the last link in the necklace chain. Pigtail the pin end right above the bicone bead.

5. Take the second tasseled eye pin and add beads in this order: filigree, pink quartz, cloisonné, bicone crystal. Attach to the other end of the necklace as in step 4.

6. To wear, tie loosely around your neck.

LIEGEOIS COCKTAIL

This bright, pretty version of the popular Belgian cocktail is perfect for an afternoon pick-me-up. Makes 1 serving.

1 shot grenadine

1 glass full of orange-flavored soda, preferably Orangina

1 orange slice, cut in half

Pour the shot of grenadine into a tall glass. Add a few ice cubes and place the orange slice on the glass rim. Then add the orange soda. Appreciate the gorgeous color scheme, then stir and drink!

tree of life

Trees are a beautiful symbol of the system Mother Earth has in place for renewing her bountiful resources. Half above the earth and half below, trees represent the balance of life. Wearing a tree symbol will remind you to stay rooted to the ground but also to reach for the sky, to approach life with both practicality and idealism. And happily, this necklace is really simple to make. It's almost like a painting, with a single tree as the focal point of the tableau.

INGREDIENTS

24 one-inch rounded beads

1 large, flat disc with two holes (mine is 2¼ x 1¼ inches)

1 gold tree charm with a flatish back

Leather cord, 2 feet long

1 gold lobster clasp

2 gold head pins

G-S Hypo Cement or any strong, clear jewelry glue

TOOLS

Round-nose pliers

Flat-nose pliers

Wire cutters

RECYCLED ELEMENTS: Blue wooden disc, amber beads from a vintage necklace

1

1. Make a loop at one end of the leather cord and tie a double knot. Add a dab of glue to the knot to secure.

2. String one bead onto the cord, then tie a knot as close to the bead as possible. (See "Knotting Between Beads," page 31.)

3

3. Add a second bead, followed by another knot. Continue adding beads and knotting between them until you've added 12 beads. After the twelfth bead, make a knot, then leave a ¼-inch space and make another knot.

4. Add another 12 beads, again separated by knots.

5. Attach a lobster clasp at the end of the beads, tying multiple knots to anchor it and adding a dab of glue to secure the knots.

APPLE WALNUT SALAD

Trees are such naturally amazing examples of productivity. Toasted walnuts are a perfect complement to juicy, crunchy red apples in this mouth-watering salad. Makes 4 servings.

1 apple, cored, cut into ½-inch cubes

½ cup chopped walnuts, toasted until slightly brown (about 1–2 minutes in toaster oven)

1 head red leaf lettuce, washed and torn into medium-sized pieces

¼ cup crumbled gorgonzola cheese

¼ cup alfalfa sprouts

¼ cup red onions, chopped thinly

Annie's Naturals Goddess Dressing

Toss all ingredients in a salad bowl and serve immediately.

7

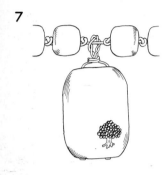

6. Take the tree charm and use wire cutters to cut off the top loop. Glue the charm to the disc with the clear glue. Let dry as recommended on the bottle.

7. My disc had two parallel holes at the top (yours might be slightly different). To attach it to the necklace, I put a head pin through each hole, bent them upward, and used pliers to twist them together over the pendant. I then looped the twisted wire together over the cord and pigtailed the ends.

long john silver

This necklace uses lots of jump rings so you can wear maximum silver with minimum effort. Silver is said to bring good luck and advantage throughout life. And really, who doesn't need as much of that as possible?

RECYCLED ELEMENTS: Shells, buttons, beads, and chain

INGREDIENTS

Navy blue leather cord, 52 inches long

70 5-mm silver jump rings

40 assorted beads and charms
(I used 9 shell beads, 2 silver whale charms, 1 silver anchor charm, 2 silver parrot charms, 4 lavender 6-mm faceted beads, 12 faceted silver 4-mm beads, 1 antique button, 2 round 8-mm green stone beads, and 3 flower beads for a nautical theme)

Figaro chain, 26 inches long (Figaro, Figaro!)

40 silver eye pins

1 silver clasp

TOOLS

Round-nose pliers

Flat-nose pliers

Wire cutters

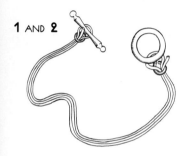

1 AND 2

3

1. Fold leather cord into three layers. Catch the loop at one end with the open ring segment of the clasp.

2. Loop the other open end of the tripled cord around the bar segment of the clasp.

3. To secure the cord ends below the clasp, use your fingers to wrap an eye pin or some 18-gauge wire around the three strands at each end, right next to the clasp. Wrap three times tightly, close together. Trim the excess with wire cutters and dull the ends of the wire by pressing it with flat-nose pliers.

4. Attach 61 jump rings to the cord using your pliers.

PIRATE'S TROPICAL TREAT

Tired of doing the laundry? Cleaning? Being a slave to the TV? Prepare to mutiny with this relaxing tropical bath concoction. Makes one bath.

2 tablespoons sea salt
Juice of ½ lime
1 small can coconut milk

As the bath runs, pour in the coconut milk, squeeze in the lime, and swish in the sea salt. Then walk the plank and commit yourself to one fabulous bath.

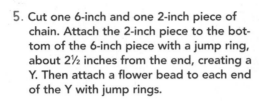

5 AND **6**

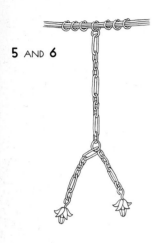

5. Cut one 6-inch and one 2-inch piece of chain. Attach the 2-inch piece to the bottom of the 6-inch piece with a jump ring, about 2½ inches from the end, creating a Y. Then attach a flower bead to each end of the Y with jump rings.

6. Find the center jump ring on your cord. Attach the Y chain, upside down, to that ring.

7. Starting from this center ring and working outward on both sides, attach something to every other jump ring. It can be a charm, bead, or segment of chain with a bead or charm attached to the end—whatever you want. You can either follow the photo or make up your own design.

7

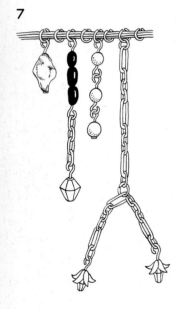

queen of hearts

I am a rococo kind of girl: more is more, and simple is boring. I love this project because it is a chance to combine tons of different colors and textures and see how they meld together. The layers and textures can be rich, deep, playful, or ethereal, depending on the beads you use. This is a good project for the color balancing test on page 16, to check for harmony and balance in the beads before you start.

INGREDIENTS

Roughly 120 assorted beads ranging from 3 to 8 mm in size
18-gauge copper wire, 1 foot (for the armature)
28-gauge copper wire, 4 yards (to wrap the armature)
Neutral-colored leather cord, 2 feet long
1 big bead or button (for the clasp)

TOOLS

2 pairs flat-nose pliers
Jewelry wire cutters
Heavy-duty wire cutters

RECYCLED ELEMENTS: Wire, many of the beads

1

1. To create the armature, cut an 8-inch piece of the heavy, 18-gauge wire. Find the halfway point and fold it about ½ inch past that point. Take the longer end and make the last inch into a loop using your flat-nose pliers. Take the shorter end and bring it to the center, then twist a loop around the bottom of the longer end so that they are connected.

2

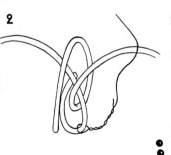

2. You're going to wrap the armature with the 28-gauge wire, stringing it with beads as you go. To attach the 28-gauge wire, wrap and twist the last inch of it onto itself, running it through a loop in the armature.

3

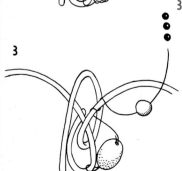

3. String a large bead on the wire to cover the twisted portion. Then wrap the wire around the armature. Add a few more beads, then wrap again. Keep stringing on beads and wrapping, moving around the armature. When you string on larger beads, just add one at a time. When you string on smaller beads, do four or five

QUEEN BEE SOAP

Wire wrapping leaves your fingers a bit black from the residue of the wire. Treat your queenly hands to a good washing with this soap, guaranteed to get the grime off.

1 tablespoon beeswax
1 cup glycerin soap base, melted
1 tablespoon honey
2 tablespoons poppy seeds
Soap mold (If you don't have a silicone soap mold, you can also use Chevre cheese containers, yogurt containers, or bologna packaging—any disposable plastic container about 3 x 4 inches will do.)

Melt the beeswax in a double boiler, then mix in the melted soap base. Add honey and stir until completely melted. Stir in the poppy seeds. Pour into mold and let harden. Release from mold. Let cure on a drying rack for a couple of days, then lather up!

at a time and wrap back around the larger beads to cover up any empty spaces. If the beads shift a bit as you wrap, pull the wire to tighten, then wrap with wire only to secure.

4

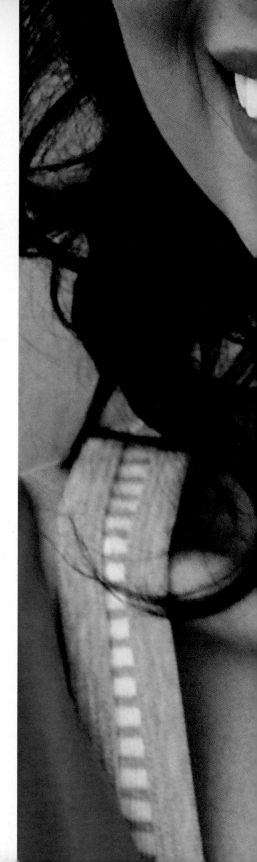

4. When you reach the end of the exposed armature, run your wire through some of the wraps you started with to secure. Then pull the wire through one of the large beads already in place and snip the wire close to the hole.

5. Add a cord by running a doubled-up length of leather through the back of the armature's loop and following the directions for making a homemade toggle clasp (page 33).

cat lady

I love cats. They are so divinely mysterious and intriguing. I adore watching them slink by as if the world were made for them. I lived at an elderly lady's apartment in Paris once and took care of her two senile cats for a year. Even though they were almost blind and constantly bumped into corners, they never seemed worried about anything, content to lie in the sun and listen to the creaks of the 200-year-old floor. This necklace is my tribute to cats—and a pretty rockin' fashion statement, too.

RECYCLED ELEMENTS: Chains from the thrift store, cameo from photographer Carrie's mom, leather cord from an old dream catcher

INGREDIENTS

1 foot black suede lace, 1/8 inch thick

1¾-inch cameo with filigree border

Heavy gold chain with large links, 18 inches long

Medium-weight gold chain, 40 inches long (I used a braided chain)

Other decorative necklaces to cut up (I used a black-and-clear beaded necklace, 11½ inches long, and an old vintage beaded necklace, 44 inches long)

11 gold jump rings

Gold lobster clasp

TOOLS

Round-nose pliers

Flat-nose pliers

Wire cutters

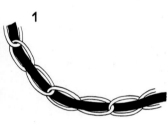

1. Take the heavy gold chain with large links and weave the suede lace through it. Loop the lace around the last link and then double the lace back through the chain, so you have two strands running through the whole chain. Trim the excess. Add the lobster clasp at one end and the clasp closure to the other end.

2. Attach the cameo to the center link with a jump ring.

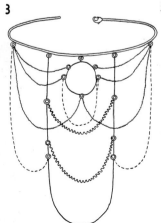

3. Cut up your decorative necklaces into various lengths and attach to the heavy chain with jump rings, following the arrangement as shown in the diagram.

HEART-O-MINE PERSONALIZED PENDANT

If you can't find a pendant that works for your project—or just want yours to feature your own sweetie (feline or otherwise)—here's how to make your own.

1 package polymer clay in a translucent or light color
Rub-on decal printer paper (see page 124 for where to find these)
Cameo back with filigree border (available at jewelry and beading stores)
G-S Hypo Cement
Clear-drying sealer or varnish

1. Roll the clay in your hands to make a round ball about the size of a quarter. Press one side gently to make a flat surface in the center of your pendant.

2. Bake the clay according to the package instructions.

3. Print or copy the image or picture of your choice onto the decal paper following package instructions, making sure it is sized to fit on the cameo (but slightly larger).

4. Rub your picture onto the clay cameo, following directions on the decal package instructions.

5. Glue the cameo to the center of the cameo base.

6. Apply a coat of sealer to protect the image and make it shine. Let dry completely.

rings, pins, and bracelets

sparkles on
a half shell

Scalloped seashells always make me think of Venus, the Roman goddess of love and beauty. Venus was immortalized in Botticelli's famous fifteenth-century painting *The Birth of Venus*, rising from the sea in a scallop shell, which was brought to my attention in the fifth grade when I noticed Jim Henson's version with Miss Piggy, of course. Seashells stimulate intuition, sensitivity, imagination, and adaptability. They also provide insight during periods of decision making—which will come in handy when deciding whether to wear this glittery tribute as a pin or a necklace.

RECYCLED ELEMENTS: Seashells, assorted beads from old jewelry

* Be sure to work in a well-ventilated area for this project, preferably outdoors. Inhaling the resin fumes is bad for your brain cells!

1. Spread a very thin layer of white glue on the inside of your shell, making sure that even the crevices in the scalloped edge are covered.

2. Pour glitter over the glue to cover the inside of the shell. Shake off excess.

3. Decide where you want your focus beads to be (think of it as a stage for your star beads). Use a toothpick to dab a few more drops of white glue on those spots.

4. Place your focus beads on the glue. Let dry for at least 20 minutes.

INGREDIENTS

Shallow half of a seashell

Seed beads, about 10

Assorted other small beads that fit in the shell

Charm with attached loop

Glitter

2-part epoxy resin, such as Envirotex Lite Coating Epoxy Resin (available at craft stores)

Disposable plastic or paper mixing cup

Popsicle stick or other mixing tool

Disposable gloves

G-S Hypo Cement or Super Glue

White glue (like Elmer's)

Toothpick

Pin back and hot glue gun (to wear it as a pin)

Chain and jump ring (to wear it as a necklace)

TOOLS

2 pairs of pliers (for necklace version only)

5. Put your gloves on and mix the resin according to the directions on the package. Pour resin into shell, filling it to the top but being careful not to let it overflow. Stabilize the shell so it's level and let cure according to the directions. The stuff is a bit stinky and mildly toxic, so work in a well-ventilated area (outside is best).

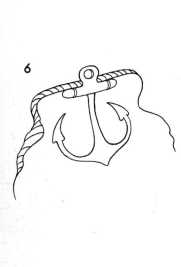

6. When the resin has cured, glue your anchor charm at the top of the shell, over the resin, with the G-S Hypo Cement or Super Glue. Make sure the charm's loop clears the top of the shell.

7. Use the hot glue gun to attach the pin back to the back of the shell. Let cool. If you'd like to wear it as a necklace instead, attach a jump ring to the charm's loop and string onto your chain.

VENUS BATH SOAK

Stimulate your inner goddess with this aromatic bath oil. Turn off your cell phone, light some candles, and treat yourself to a long, luxurious soak! Makes one splendid bath.

- 3 cinnamon sticks
- 2 tablespoons fresh ground ginger
- 12 tablespoons sea salt
- 4 drops bergamot essential oil
- 2 tablespoons honey
- 1 tablespoon glitter body lotion (to make the bubbles shimmer)

Combine all ingredients in a bowl. Pour into a hot bath, climb in, and feel immortal.

festival of
lanterns bracelet

I love lanterns because they make me think of summertime parties and Chinatown, two of my favorite things. The key ingredients in this charmingly thick, heavy bracelet are the filigree beads, bead caps, and crowns; the chain tassels that make it look lanternesque; and the cloisonné beads, which give the "lanterns" a special glow.

RECYCLED ELEMENTS: Chain from thrift-store bracelet, beads from old jewelry

INGREDIENTS

16 large beads in assorted colors and shapes (round, disc, and oval)

10 cloisonné beads

5 7-mm gold filigree beads

18 seed beads or 4-mm crystals

6 15-mm gold filigree bead caps

4 5-mm gold filigree bead caps

4 4-mm gold filigree bead caps

24 gold eye pins

Heavy gold chain, 8 inches long (for the bracelet)

Thinner gold chain, 15 inches long (for the tassels; I used a cable chain)

2 jump rings

Gold toggle clasp

TOOLS

Round-nose pliers

Flat-nose pliers

Wire cutters

1

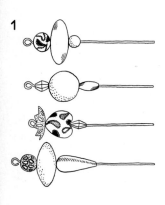

1. Arrange the beads and bead caps on eye pins in a variety of combinations, as shown in accompanying illustration.

2. Take the thin, 15-inch chain and use wire cutters to snip it into 15 equal pieces, each 1 inch long. These will be your tassels.

3. Decorate 5 of your beaded eye pins with tassels. To do this, use your pliers to open the loop on the end of each eye pin. Attach 3 chain pieces, then close the loop.

3

4. Leaving those pins decorated with cloisonné beads aside for now, attach the other beaded pins to the bracelet. To attach, loop the pin through a link in the chain and pigtail the pin end.

5

5. Now attach the pins with cloisonné beads to the bracelet every ¼ inch on alternating sides of the chain, again using the pigtailing method.

6. Attach a jump ring to each end of the bracelet chain and then attach the 2 pieces of the toggle clasp to opposite ends.

SESAME GLOW FOOT POLISH

Slather this mixture over your feet to smooth and moisturize. Then slip on a pair of strappy sandals, head to Chinatown, and dance the night away under magical lit lanterns.

4 tablespoons sesame seeds
4 tablespoons honey
2 tablespoons fresh ground ginger
3 drops lemon juice

Combine all ingredients in a bowl. Scrub feet vigorously with the concoction and leave on for 10 minutes. After washing away, feet will feel soft and invigorated.

bohemian
wrapsody ring

This ring has the bohemian woman in mind—the kind who likes her fingers dressed up with a just a hint of sweet excess. A fast, easy wire-wrapping project that gives you dramatic results with a nostalgic flair, this project makes a great gift for your indulgent side.

INGREDIENTS

- 25 assorted glass beads, plastic beads, and seed beads, 3–6 mm each
- 18-gauge wire, 6 inches long (for the ring element) or ring base with small platform
- 28-gauge wire, 2 feet long

TOOLS

- 2 pairs flat-nose pliers
- Jewelry wire cutters
- Heavy-duty wire cutters

RECYCLED ELEMENTS: Wire, beads

1

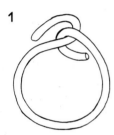

1. If you're making the ring base from 18-gauge wire, follow the diagram shown here to form the ring armature. Measure the finger you wish to wear it on and then make the armature about ⅛ inch bigger than that: adding the wire-wrapped beads will reduce the area that your finger will fit through.

3

2. Attach the 28-gauge wire to your armature or ring base by twisting the last ½ inch of the wire together on one side of the front loop of the ring.

3. You're now going to wrap the armature with the 28-gauge wire, stringing it with beads as you go. String on one or two beads at a time, then run the wire through the bead cluster back around the front. You're basically beading across the top ½ inch of the ring, back and forth, and building up that area. Leave the rest of the armature plain as the ring band.

4

4. When you're finished, wrap the wire through the beads and weave it in and out of the beaded buildup. Tuck your wire into a bead with a bigger hole and pull it through. Use a wire cutter to trim any excess.

BOHEMIAN CUCUMBER YOGURT DIP

Serve this flavorful dip at your next free-spirited gathering with pita chips or chunks of bread. Your guests will adore munching on the crunchy, sweet, and tangy dip. Wear your ring and show off your impressive culinary skills and craftiness! Serves 6–8

- 1 cup plain, lowfat yogurt
- Half a cucumber, peeled and cubed
- Pinch of salt
- Dash of cool water
- 2 tablespoons finely sliced walnuts
- 2 tablespoons dried black currants
- 2 tablespoons finely chopped mint

With a fork, whip together the yogurt, water, salt, and cucumbers. Garnish with walnuts, black currants, and mint and serve with pita or bread.

in-the-spotlight ring

There is nothing more dramatic than a single, large stone. The trick with this project is to use a well-cut, evenly faceted oval stone that can hold its own in the spotlight. The hot-pink stone I used is pink phantom quartz, said to stimulate the heart chakra and help you approach your goals confidently. The alternative stone in lavender is, believe it or not, plastic!

RECYCLED ELEMENT: Stone from broken earrings

INGREDIENTS

1 faceted oval gemstone, 15 mm wide (or any bead about that size)

24-gauge gold wire, 1 yard long

TOOLS

Wire cutters

DRAMA QUEEN PINK LEMONADE

This pink lemonade is bright and sweet enough to grab the spotlight at any gathering. Makes 6 servings.

1 cup prickly pear juice
½ cup lemon juice
½ cup sugar
2 cups sparkling water
Ice cubes

Mix prickly pear juice, lemon juice, and sugar in a blender. Pour ¼ cup of the mixture into a tall glass over ice and add ⅓ cup sparkling water. Stir well and serve.

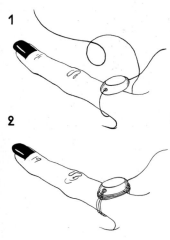

1

2

1. Run the wire through the bead and then wrap it around the base of your finger to measure the ring base, leaving an 18-inch tail on one end and about two feet at other end.

2. Using the 2-foot-long tail of the wire, run three more loops around your finger and through the bead, if the bead's hole permits. If the wire only fits through the hole once or twice, run the wire under the bead to thicken up the band. Wrap the wire three times around each side of the stone to secure it.

3. Take the 18-inch tail of the wire and start wrapping it around the face of the bead several times, forming a loose but structured circular formation around the bead.

4

4b

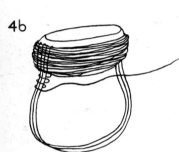

5

4. When there are about 8 inches of wire left, pull it through all the wraps on one side of the bead to grab and hold all the wires together, as in a bundle, and wrap around the bundle three times. Then run the wire around to the other side of the bead and do the same to that group of wires.

5. Pull wire back through the hole of the bead, if there is enough room, and finish by wrapping the remaining wire three times around all the wires.

cozy nest ring

INGREDIENTS

3   3-mm oval pearl beads

28-gauge gold or silver wire, 1 yard long

1   ring base with round, flat, ½-inch-wide platform

TOOLS

Flat-nose pliers

Wire cutters

Birds build nests to have homes where they can warm their eggs safely and discreetly, protected from the elements. Wearing a nest on your finger brings a certain homey instinct to the forefront of your thoughts, too—a cozy fire, friends, family, laughter, and fun.

FOUND ELEMENTS: Pearls from an old necklace

1. Twist tie the first inch of the wire around the arm of the ring at the base of the platform.

2. Wrap the tied wire around the base three times and bring the wire up across the platform.

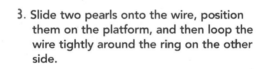

3. Slide two pearls onto the wire, position them on the platform, and then loop the wire tightly around the ring on the other side.

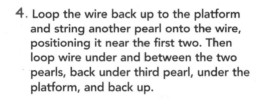

4. Loop the wire back up to the platform and string another pearl onto the wire, positioning it near the first two. Then loop wire under and between the two pearls, back under third pearl, under the platform, and back up.

5

5. Encircle the three pearls with the wire in rounds to create a nest around the eggs. Wrap tightly at first, then more loosely to build a thick wall.

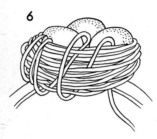

6

6. Weave the wire under the mass of wires and across the nest, then under the platform, back up, under the nest at a different point, and across the pearls, securing the wire to the platform. Check the nest as you go to make sure that it is being secured to the platform.

7. Run wire across the nest, weaving it around the circumference. Leave just enough wire to insert the end deep into the nest with your flat-nose pliers, tucking it into the interior space around the pearls.

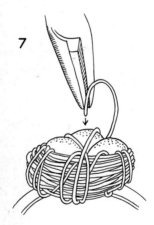

7

RECIPE FOR A COZY NEST

I am the cozy nest queen, loving nothing better than hanging out at home with my girlfriends. Here is my favorite recipe for a night in with the gals.

1 pot chai tea (see below)
1 box Walkers shortbread cookies
1 DVD (*Bridget Jones's Diary* or another chick flick)
1 deck tarot cards
7 terrible jokes
Pillows and really big blankets
3 good friends

CHAI TEA

This recipe makes two servings, so multiply as many times as you have guests.

⅓ cup water
3-4 cardamom pods
A few cloves
A few black peppercorns
A few pods allspice

¼ cup fresh ginger root, chopped
⅔ cup 2% milk
1 teaspoon loose black tea (plus a bit extra)
Sugar to taste

1. Add spices and water in a saucepan. Bring to a boil, then remove from heat and let steep for 5 to 20 minutes, depending on how strong a spice flavor you want.

2. Pour in the milk. Bring the mixture just to a boil and remove from heat.

3. Add the tea. Let steep for 5 to 10 minutes to taste. (If you want, reheat to a simmer after it steeps, then remove from heat.) You can add sugar at this point, or serve without sugar and let people add their own. Traditionally, sugar is added before serving.

4. Strain into a pot. Serve.

extra goodies

mystery
owl bookmark

There is nothing better than curling up on the couch with a novel that takes you far, far away. But then . . . you must get up and go to the bathroom once in a while. What do you use as a bookmark? A scraggly piece of newspaper? A sad, crumpled tissue? Instead, make a simple, precious bookmark with an old chain and a few charms in a matter of minutes. It makes a great present, too!

RECYCLED ELEMENT: Chain

1. Attach a jump ring to one end of the chain and then attach a charm to the ring.

2. Attach 3 jump rings to the other end and attach 1 charm to each ring.

INGREDIENTS

4 gold charms (I used an owl, Big Ben, a cup of tea, and a crown)
Gold chain, 10 inches long (I used a box chain)
4 gold jump rings

TOOLS

Flat-nose pliers
A second pair of pliers
Wire cutters (only if the chain needs shortening)

MOROCCAN MINT TEA

Here's a delicious mint tea to sip while you're reading. Use your new bookmark to hold your spot while you pour! Makes 1 pot, or 4 cups.

12 fresh mint sprigs, plus 3 more for garnish
3 teaspoons green tea
2 tablespoons raw sugar
4 cups water

Boil water. Combine the mint, green tea, and sugar in a teapot (or any pot with a lid) and then fill with the hot water. Cover and let tea brew, stirring the leaves once or twice, for 3 minutes. Pour tea through a tea strainer into glass teacups to serve. Garnish with remaining sprigs of mint.

daisy
gardening boots

Daisies have such pretty connotations. The Irish say that dreaming of daisies at the beginning of spring brings months of good luck. They also say that to dream of your love, place your shoes (or rubber boots, in this case) outside the door to your room and put daisy roots under your pillow. This sounds a bit dirty, but I tried it and it actually worked!

RECYCLED ELEMENT: Boots

INGREDIENTS

1   pair rubber boots (available at most hardware stores)

16 fabric daisy appliqués

Approximately sixty 3-mm yellow seed beads

Green rickrack ribbon, 1 yard long

1   can pink spray paint (I used Krylon H20 paint in Rhine River Red)

Mustard yellow craft paint

E6000 glue

Small brush or sponge

Fabric glue

TOOLS

Small paintbrush

Scissors

Toothpick

1. Spray-paint the boots following directions on the can. Be sure to put down plenty of old newspaper and to do this outside or in a well-ventilated area.

2. Use fabric glue to attach 8 daisy appliqués onto each boot, making sure to cover the backs of the daisies entirely with glue.

3. Place a generous dab of glue in the center of each daisy and pour seed beads onto the glue, pressing them down so they sink in.

4. Paint the toe and the top trim of each boot with yellow paint.

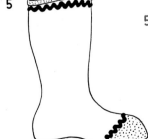

5. Glue the green ribbon around the top edge of each boot and along the toe line, as shown. Let dry at least overnight before wearing. (These are okay to wear in light rain, but you may risk losing a few beads if worn in a serious downpour.)

DAISY-CHAIN WREATH

To make a daisy chain, pick a bunch of daisies and use your fingernail to pierce a hole in each stem, toward the base of the flower. Thread one stem through the hole in another until stopped by the head of the flower. Repeat until you have a chain long enough for a simple bracelet, wreath, and/or necklace. Put on and dance in a field, like Isadora Duncan.

old-time
button headband

Buttons have long constituted more than just a way to fasten clothes. The first duke of Buckingham had a suit and cloak covered with diamond buttons. I must admit, I understand the passion. Buttons can make an outfit fantastic, and I always notice well-made buttons on a garment. This project is great for showcasing vintage buttons collecting dust in a bottle or tin somewhere. The old ones seem to carry the most charm.

RECYCLED ELEMENTS: Buttons from an old box of buttons

INGREDIENTS

18–25 small- and medium-sized buttons (I used buttons in neutral shades, but you can use any colors you like)

Thin leather cord, 2 feet long (I used silver cord; use whatever color matches your buttons)

Elastic, 5 mm wide and 12 inches long

TOOLS

Scissors

2

3

1. Arrange the buttons in any order you prefer.

2. Fold the leather cord in half and make a double-knot with a ½-inch loop at the doubled end.

3. String the cord through each button in turn, staggering them so they overlap slightly. If a button has four holes, use both strands of the cord to make an X through the holes. If a button has two holes, use just one strand and run the other strand behind the button. If a button has a loop on its back, make an X through it with the leather strands so the button stays straight.

4. When you have about 3 inches left of the cord, make a loop and tie a triple knot.

5. Take your elastic and tie it to one of the looped ends of your leather cord. Pull it through the other loop and try the headband on, pulling the elastic until the headband fits snugly. Mark with your finger where the elastic hits the loop and tie it at that point. Trim the excess.

PEACH BUTTON COOKIES

These adorable cookies look just like little peaches and are the perfect accompaniment to afternoon tea with cucumber sandwiches. Take tea while wearing your button headband and your prettiest sundress.

¾ cup sweet butter
½ cup whole milk
1 cup sugar
2 eggs
1 tsp baking powder
3¾ cups all-purpose flour
1 tsp vanilla extract
⅔ cup apricot jam
¼ cup chocolate pieces, melted and cooled

⅓ cup ground pecans
2 tsp sherry or rum
¼ cup water
⅓ cup red sugar
⅔ cup yellow-orange sugar
Whole candied mint, lemon balm, lemon verbena leaves, violets, borage, or rose petals for garnish

1. Preheat oven to 325 degrees.

2. Blend the butter, milk, sugar, eggs, baking powder, and 2 cups of the flour with an electric mixer on low for 1 minute, scraping down the bowl constantly. Increase to medium speed and beat one minute more, continuing to scrape down the bowl.

3. Stir in the remaining flour and the vanilla.

4. Shape dough into smooth ¾-inch balls (each ball will make half a peach). Place balls one inch apart on lightly greased cookie sheet.

5. Bake until are cookies brown on the bottom, about 15-20 minutes. Remove and cool on a wire rack.

6. Place the tip of a small knife in the center of each cookie and carefully rotate to make a hollow. Reserve the crumbs that fall off in a bowl.

7. Mix the crumbs (about 1½ cups) with jam, chocolate, nuts, and rum. Fill the hollowed cookies with the crumb mixture.

8. Press the flat sides of two filled cookies together gently to resemble a peach.

9. Brush each "peach" lightly with water and then immediately roll one side in red sugar, for blush.

10. Sprinkle yellow-orange sugar on each "peach," covering them completely.

11. Add your whole candied leaves as your peach stems. *Voilà!*

i ♥ sailors tee

This project is a whimsical combination of sailor shirt and one side of a beaded coin purse. If the coin purse is beaded on both sides, you could make two shirts, or a matching dog jacket for your pooch.

RECYCLED ELEMENTS: Coin purse, shirt

INGREDIENTS
Striped sailor shirt
Beaded, red heart-shaped coin purse
Red lace, twice the circumference of the coin purse
Sewing needle and red thread
Pins

TOOLS
Scissors
Seam ripper

1. Use the seam ripper to carefully detach the seams of the coin purse, starting with the side opening.

2

2. Pin the beaded heart in place on the shirt. Then pin the lace around the outside of the heart, ruffling it as you go. Finish by turning the ruffle under where the lace overlaps itself.

3. Thread the needle. Sew the heart to the shirt, poking the needle through from the wrong side and using a straight stitch to go around the perimeter of the heart, catching the lace under the edge of the heart with each stitch.

3

4. Finish by securely knotting the thread at the back of the shirt. Always wash this shirt by hand to ensure that the beaded part stays intact.

POPEYE'S FAMOUS SPINACH

Need extra strength for a night on the town? Just whip up this healthy side dish and you'll be strong as a sailor. Makes 2 servings.

1 12-oz. bag prewashed fresh spinach
Juice of half a lemon
2 cloves garlic
Pinch of salt
½ cup olive oil

Heat the oil in a wok or frying pan over medium-high heat. Crush the garlic and sauté in the heated oil. When the garlic is soft but not brown, add the spinach and salt. Sauté until cooked (about 3 minutes). Squeeze lemon to taste and serve.

lucky clover
hair comb

Celtic knots are such beautiful shapes in their symmetry and unending form. They are a reminder of the symmetrical shape of a clover. Apparently, there is one four-leaf clover for every ten thousand three-leaf clovers. I've been looking all my life, and I still haven't found a single one.

RECYCLED ELEMENTS: Wire, beads, hair comb

INGREDIENTS

Roughly 100 assorted beads ranging from 3 mm to 10 mm

18-gauge wire, 1 foot long (for the armature)

28-gauge wire, 4 feet long (for wrapping)

2-inch hair comb

TOOLS

2 pairs flat-nose pliers

Jewelry wire cutters

Heavy-duty wire cutters

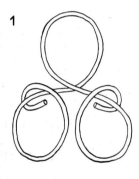

1

1. Take the heavy, 18-gauge wire and gently bend and shape it to create an armature for the decoration, following the diagram shown here. The final bent shape should be about 2 inches wide by 2 inches long.

2. You're going to wrap the finished armature with the 28-gauge wire, stringing it with beads as you go. Follow steps 2–4 for the Queen of Hearts Necklace (page 78) for instructions. When you finish wrapping the armature, you should still have at least 1 foot of 28-gauge wire left.

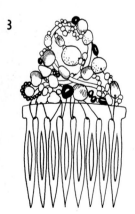

3

3. Place the armature against the comb, with the botom of the armature overlapping the comb part by about ½ inch. Take the excess wire and use it to attach the armature to the top edge of the comb. Starting at one end, wrap it circularly around the teeth of the comb and around the armature, pulling tightly as you go.

4. Finish by circling wire around the other end of the comb and running the wire through a bead before snipping off any excess.

LUCKY GINGER LEMON ELIXIR

This sweet, sour, and spicy drink is so tasty and invigorating, it gets the blood flowing and puts a spring in your step. It will certainly wake you up to finding those lucky clovers! Makes 2 servings.

2 cups water
¼ cup fresh ginger, chopped
Juice of 1 lemon
2 tablespoons honey

Add the water and ginger to a saucepan and simmer for 20 minutes. Strain off ginger pieces. Add lemon and honey to the water. Pour into glasses and serve with cookies.

reigning
precious tiara

Unless you happen to be a real princess (and not just your daddy's), a tiara is one of those things you will probably only get to wear once or twice in your lifetime. So why not have one standing at the ready? This project isn't too hard, but it takes a while; plan on a good week or two of nightly rendezvous with your bowl of beads. The finshed product is such a fanciful jewel and definitely worth the effort!

RECYCLED ELEMENTS: Beads, hair combs, wire

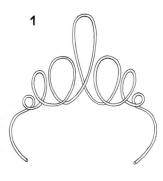

1. Take the heavy, 18-gauge wire and shape it to create an armature for the tiara. Bend it in half to create the first loop, keeping the bent end rounded, then follow the diagram shown here.

2. You're going to wrap the armature with the 28-gauge wire, stringing it with beads as you go. Follow steps 2–4 for the Queen of Hearts Necklace (page TK) for instructions.

3. Add the hair combs by wrapping the ends of the tiara and the combs together with 28-gauge wire. Make sure the front sides of the combs are facing out and that the teeth are facing down. Run the ends of the wire through the beads so they don't poke your head.

4. Secure the tiara on your favorite princess!

INGREDIENTS

Roughly 600 assorted beads, ranging from 3 mm to 6 mm

18-gauge wire, 2½ feet long (for the armature)

28-gauge wire, 8 yards long (for wrapping)

2 2-inch hair combs

TOOLS

2 pairs flat-nose pliers

Jewelry wire cutters

Heavy-duty wire cutters

PRINCESS PINK FROSTING

This is the sweetest, lightest frosting to top your favorite cupcakes or perhaps one big royal cake. Heavenly, sweet, and creamy, it's fit only for the most delicate of tastebuds.

1 box powdered sugar
¼ cup plus 1 tablespoon whole milk
   Dash of vanilla extract
1 stick sweet cream butter, cut into ¼-inch cubes
1 drop red food coloring with a tiny hint of blue food coloring

Mix the first three ingredients together in a mixer on high speed with a whisk attachment, adding the cubes of butter as the mixture melds. Add the food coloring last: Dip the tip of a toothpick into the red dye and stir it into the frosting so you don't use too much; use the other end of the toothpick to stir in the hint of blue.

acknowledgments

Thank you to the crew that made this book fabulous: Dany Paragouteva, a truly talented illustrator; Carrie Grim, for her fresh photography; Kate Couture, for making all the girls so pretty; Gina M., for styling the shoots; and art director Jamie Dean, for the tile and shingled backdrops. Thanks to the team at Watson-Guptill that worked so hard on it as well: Julie Mazur, Amy Vinchesi, L49 Design, Andrea Glickson, and Nicole Miller. Special thanks to Urban Outfitters and Anthropologie for many of the great clothes that made the book so stylish. Thanks to the models: Sarah M. Scott, Kenisha, Crystal, and Brenda Hernandez. And special thanks to Deb Warren, my lit agent, for her support and guidance.

Finally, thanks to my friends and family, and to my soulmate, Christop.

resource guide

The art of bling is alive and well. This means that there are tons of places to get supplies for jewelry making—you just have to look around your area or online. Here are the resources I used for projects in this book.

BEADS, BEADING TOOLS, WIRE, AND JEWELRY FINDINGS

Beadalon

Beadalon makes great jewelry tools, beads, and every finding imaginable. Search their website for a retailer near you.
www.beadalon.com

Beads and Charms

Web-only retailer of beading and jewelry supplies.
www.beadsandcharms.com

Beads & More

My pearls for the Cozy Nest Ring are from here.

800 South Maple Street, Suite A
Los Angeles, CA 90014
(213) 955-9000

Berger Specialty Company, Inc.

A great selection of cameos, charms, seed beads, wire, ring forms, leather cord, chains, and everything else.

413 East Eighth Street
Los Angeles, CA 90014
(213) 627-8783
www.bergerbeads.net

BJ Craft Supplies

Online retailer of craft supplies.
www.bjcraftsupplies.com

Bohemian Crystal

All charms used in this book except the vintage ones are from here.

810 South Maple Avenue
Los Angeles, CA 90014
(213) 624-2121
www.beadsfactory.com

C&C International

This is where I got the fantastic faceted moonstone and pink quartz for the Bright Pretty Things Lariat, the green jade beads for the Fresh Cherry Drop Earrings, and the Purple Power faceted teardrops.

101 Utah Street, Suite 103
San Francisco, CA 94103
(408) 373-8663
lauraysun@yahoo.com

EE Beads

Online resource for jewelry supplies.
www.eebeads.com

Jo-Ann Fabric and Crafts Store

Huge selection of craft supplies and fabric. Check website for a location near you.
www.joann.com

Michaels

Craft megastore. Check website for a location near you.
www.michaels.com

Plaid Industries

Plaid makes great beads that are available at bead and craft stores everywhere. Check their website for a retailer near you.
www.plaidonline.com

Bel Rub-On Decals

Rub-on decals can be used for the Cat Lady personalized pendant.
www.rubondecals.com

FOR USED AND VINTAGE FINDS

Goodwill Industries
www.goodwill.org

Salvation Army
www.salvationarmy.org

American Cancer Association Discovery Shops
www.cancer.org

index